Return to what remains

Kavita Ivy Nandan

Return to what remains

Acknowledgements

The following poems were previously published:
'An empty beach' in *Mindfood*, March 2021
'Words on the pavement' in *LiteLitOne*, January 2021
'Nani' in *Not Very Quiet*, 14 September 2020

For my parents, who never stop believing in me, largely because they are my mum and dad.

For Michael and Jesse, my lockdown companions.
We survived, despite living on top of each other (literally).

Return to what remains
ISBN 978 1 76109 389 0
Copyright © Kavita Ivy Nandan 2022
Cover image: Michael Kosmider

First published 2022 by
GINNINDERRA PRESS
PO Box 3461 Port Adelaide 5015
www.ginninderrapress.com.au

Contents

Preface	7
To sleep, perchance to dream	13
An empty beach	15
Bad dreams	16
Unveiled	17
Big, bare universities	18
Death to the extrovert	19
Hitting the high notes	20
A lust for life	21
Raincoat	22
When they met again	24
Home schooling	26
What should we do now?	28
1,2,3,4 school kids	29
Words on the pavement	30
Blue skies	34
In lockdown	35
Bat wing	37
Shooting star	38
Nani	39
Daffodils	41
Family WhatsApp	42
Fred Hollows' gully	43
Woman in the park	45
Angel	46
Eight squares of stained glass	47
Vertigo	48
Never before	49
Playing Robinson Crusoe	50

Two Haiku	51
We are all in this together	52
Do the hokey pokey	53
A normal day	54
Takeaway pie with tomato sauce	55
Return to what remains	56

Preface

On 25 January 2020, the first case in Australia of the novel Coronavirus (2019-nCoV) was confirmed. A man from Wuhan flew to Melbourne from Guangdong. One man, one flight and our lives transformed, mutated – not from a world war, a civil war or natural disaster – from a virus. Today (26 October 2021) there are 130,000 cases of Covid-19 in Australia and 1,448 deaths. Tomorrow there will be more.

Nineteen months after that first case, Australia's states and territories closed their borders to each other and enforced hard and swift lockdowns, imposing a ring of steel around the worst-hit state, New South Wales, inadvertently also around themselves: we were both locked out and locked in. By 11 October, Sydney had been in lockdown for 107 days.

This time the outbreak started in the eastern suburbs of Sydney where I live (before that, it was in the northern beaches) and then the virus spread westward. Greater Sydney was subject to stay-at-home orders and a curfew in some parts. The radius in which we shopped for food, exercised and sought medical attention shrank from ten to five kilometres. The police and army patrolled hotspots to ensure that we were complying. At a later date, if you did not live in one of the local government areas of concern and were doubly vaccinated, you were allowed to picnic with five other adults. The New South Wales premier dangled the vaccination carrot for weeks, only the percentages changed, 50, 60, 70, 80. Understandably, we became obsessed with numbers. Gladys Berejiklian's daily press conference at 11 a.m. marked time in a period where we lost track of time – the weekdays merged into the weekend, one day into the other.

Lockdowns are hard. There is a great deal of anxiety to contend with – worry about family and friends that we can't be physically near and about our spouses and children who are here in body but much like ourselves, disoriented, lost in some kind of heavy mist. These things are still bearable, though, because they are not permanent; less so is the thought of any of them being infected by the virus. We are also feeling sorrow for a world that, along with the virus, faces the challenges of multiple environmental disasters and humanitarian crises. The first lockdown was a shock to the system but seeing an endpoint got us through. The second lockdown was more agonising because it became more and more difficult to see the end, not only of future lockdowns but of the virus itself that continues to mutate.

On a more cheerful note, this second time round, I learnt how to bake bread for the first time (not very well), tried new recipes and home-schooled my child with a little more class. My friends, some with a glass of wine in their hand, told me on Facebook and Facetime that they were taking up crochet, knitting and painting. Hands are great healers of the heart's anxieties.

For my relatives in Delhi, finding paths to healing has been more challenging. Some of them caught the virus and are still recovering from it. All of them have been living with the realities of extraordinary numbers of infection and death, especially during the second wave of the pandemic. Now they are waiting with dread for the third. During Delhi's worst period, I wondered what my relatives were feeling and thinking all those millions of kilometres away. As I walked on the rocks at Clovelly in the evenings and watched the peninsula light up, were my aunts, uncles and cousins standing by the windows of their houses and watching the glowing light from burning pyres? Or worse, had they witnessed the actual pyres? The places we commonly walk in Sydney – parks and sidewalks – in their city had mutated into spaces for burning thousands of people killed by the virus. These are not things about which one can easily ask. There have been periods of complete silence on our family WhatsApp, especially in April when infections and deaths peaked. Thankfully, an insistent pinging like a regular heartbeat would begin again: my relatives posting images of birthday celebrations in lockdown, plants growing in the garden, lyrics of a song. Whatever it takes to feel human again, I suppose.

For me, a way through has been writing poetry. It is poetry's precision of image, word, line, space and indent that enters deeply; it enables connection with that precious moment in time and space and offers lasting resonance for our lives. It is that sublime space that inspires us to be creative with language. Truthful too, in our reflection on what we as human beings can, at the end of the day, hold onto in a time like this – love, friendship and our rich, mutable imaginations.

During this pandemic, I have visited Albie Smith Memorial and Baker parks, Coogee and Clovelly beaches – two of the closest parks and beaches to my house, phoned, Facetimed and Zoomed my family and friends, Whatsapped my school mother's group, ordered online from Harris Farms, Coles, Woolies, Naked Wines, followed Marley Spoon and Go Fresh recipes, loaded the dishwasher, changed from morning to evening pyjamas and listened to the 11 a.m. NSW press conference what seems like hundreds of times. I have also written thirty-three poems about living in the time of Covid-19. It feels like an achievement because, before this, I had not written poetry for at least two decades. The book includes poems written during the early days of the pandemic when case numbers and mortality rates around the world were smaller and we were in a state of surprise. Sometimes, it feels like a haunting refrain about lockdown, isolation and home schooling. The poems also suggest hints of some new reality evolving in the wilderness that we are being asked to negotiate – perhaps there is light at the end of the tunnel.

Four years ago, I moved from Canberra to Coogee with my partner and my son, who is seven years old now and has experienced two birthdays in lockdown. I have found living near the ocean to be a wonderful experience. For me, it carries memories of growing up by the sea in Fiji; a place of paradise, then loss after coups and migration. For this reason, I have included in this book a poem not directly about Covid-19, but one that reflects a time that shaped me, my thinking and a time when I needed to search for strength. This complex experience of childhood is now oddly comforting to recall when we are being asked to be resilient once more, during an extended period of lockdown and in the face of our new 'freedom' of living with the virus. I have derived a sense of comfort from thinking that Canberra and Fiji have relatively low numbers of the virus but, with fluctuating infections, I realise that there are no safe spaces out there, only in us.

I have always noticed that people look especially joyful swimming in the ocean. What could be more beautiful than watching your grandmother, who had made the journey on her own from Delhi to Suva, smiling brightly as she lifts her newly purchased pink Fijian mumu, revealing broad, brown knees – knees that I have inherited – as she walks into the calm and warm waters of Deuba beach in Suva. I have included a poem about her in this book because there are some people in your life who are too glorious to leave out. I understand now more than ever that my writing arises out of all of it – my past, my present and my inability to envision my future with confidence.

Nearly forty years later, I have loved watching my partner jump in the fresh, high waves at Coogee with my thrilled son and people of all ages and sizes frolicking on the beach surrounded by the primal cliffs of the peninsula. When Covid-19 first struck, the beach was empty and cordoned off like a sad and strange apparition. In the second lockdown, we were permitted to return to the beach for exercise; some people felt comfortable enough to be here briefly. We caught glimpses of each other's sober and grateful faces before scurrying back home. These restrictions were limiting but it felt as if they might also be freeing because they made us look inwards. It was almost like being given a gift that you weren't sure you wanted, at first. Much like unmasked faces have became more lovable because, for a time there, we were in danger of forgetting not only each other's faces but our own. There is much longing in these poems and, I do wish, also hope.

To sleep, perchance to dream

You fall asleep on nights
that feel like extended days
or the other way around.
Wake suddenly
but are not awake –
forgetting you are living
the days of Covid-19.

The mind swan
               dives
off time
into an obsidian ocean
drowns in fathoms of timelessness,
breaching for air.

Dreamy eyes are dazzled by
huts huddled together in the
glittering heat of a peninsula
lost in internet interconnectivity
creativity too; children constructing
shaky shelters from boxes of
Marley Spoon, Naked Wines:
gourmandised living at your doorstep
masking boredom and despair
that can go nowhere
like anger, the kind
that makes you punch a horse.

The heart is cowardly, yet
can recall better times, open spaces, faraway places
before we are, once again,
back in bed –
no sleeping or dreaming
but acutely aware
of lockdown.

An empty beach

there's nothing so lonesome
than a pub with no beer
Slim says

but

an empty beach
is most beautiful
I think

seagulls stroll free
from shrieking hands
bluebottles do the backstroke
in an open sea
the sun purports no purpose, least of all
to boil folks, and
the sand relaxes
with no weight
upon it

while a person curls like a mollusc
on a concrete step cordoned off.

Bad dreams

Last night I dreamt
Of fruit; harmless things
In a time like this.

Pomegranate packed with units of blood
A date like a dried organ.
The fig's arterial chamber.

The next morning
Gathering the three,
They still had power over me.

Red liquid squirted on my blouse,
Fibrous flesh messed up my lips,
A heart collapsed in my fingers.

Unveiled

    They say the eyes are the windows of the soul
    But I miss your nose
    Oblong, menhir misfit
Sightly left of centre,
    Different from the rest
    'Tis the bridge to either side of your bespoke face:

One half smooth   the other rough
like seawater pebbles   like wild weather

And those lips sulking behind
breathable tarp
muttering like a damned fool.

You are an
escarpment scaffolded
AWAITING REPAIRS
But when you are alone
put away the mask
fall in love all over again with
your exquisite face.

Big, bare universities

Chairs stacked, shrouds placed
Over objects as if they were secrets
This café is closed and the next
Where have all the students gone?
Far, far away!

Imprints of the living left behind in
Murals of the imagination
Spray-painted on the walls

Disembodied voices have taken over
The drone of the AC, the hum of fridges
Is that a cough on campus?
Swallowed by the vacuum

In the wilderness of a big university
My heart picks up
When I notice small life:
A bird in the bushes
A quivering plant

The Eye of Providence watches
Over us and doesn't even ask
What will humanity do next?

The many-headed gorgon
Boasts buildings of Medicine, Science, Business
But experiences the loneliness of medusa
Venomous virus.

Death to the extrovert

800 dying a day in Italy
800 in Spain
140,000 predicted to die in Indonesia
240,000 in America
India we dare not hazard a guess – spraying with bleach
might do for the moment
Or create another curve.

Can you spare a moment for the eastern suburb ladies?
Acclimatised to jaunty walks down Coogee Bay Road
Little point to their false lashes and Botox now
Gone is the Greek chorus and the lapping lads.

Drink to the drag queens
Most performative of the lot
The wigs, the tape, psychedelic make-up
No audience in sight.

But it's really the extrovert, like myself, who suffers most
No one to flash a winning smile to
No reason to invent a conversation
To spark a flame, to warm the heart of stranger or friend
Now we're sitting at home, strangest to ourselves,
Performing all alone.

Hitting the high notes

Slumbering at 10.15 a.m.
In lockdown again
I heard a scream
A high-pitched sort of thing
Like an opera singer controlling a high note
There it was again
I sat up in bed
Imagining a girl-child
Running through the family home, now a prison
Her knotty hair afloat
Her raging hands ajar
No longer standable
Understandable
I got up and did the vacuuming
Making a noise of my own.

A lust for life

for Marcelle

A red scarf
winds around your head – a luminous globe –
sealing cracks
that get wider.

Feet teeter on the last step
hands reaching for the rusty railing
hard enough
to crack the skull.

The world fills with sadness
as you sleep alone
sun breaching plane trees
your children lost – like infinite others –
in London and Hong Kong.

For that hour
we sit close together
reading each other's lips
your ivory spun hair
swirling in cups of Earl Grey
we talk excitedly about books
Boyd unfettered in the background
making idle gossip about people we hardly know –
your lust for life
keeping you, and me
alive.

Raincoat

Your mother fierce with ambition
waits by the steely gate
for you – baby turned schoolboy too soon.
The rain falls steadily; curling her hair, wetting her lips.

Two by two, the children released
race into their parents' embrace.
Finally you appear
Like a mirage in the distance – untouchable –
circling, chasing your tail like a cat
uncooperative raincoat!

Turning, turning in the maddening gyre.

She stops herself from subverting
new laws of social distance,
trespassing school territory.
She waits and watches
her emotions monsoonal
your hands small and fumbling, finally
raincoat on!

Speeding towards her with
oversized bag, lunch box falling out
she tumbles
remembering her mother
and her father, who warned,
'Don't tell her all your sorrows.'
But I never listened
Because she was the best listener
she has the biggest heart
and only now I understand.

My aches were growing-up pains –
passages from innocence to experience.
Now I feel a parent's pain
that will not wash out in the rain
as I turn his raincoat outside in.

When they met again

On one square
At the top of the outside stairs
His side of the fence
The exact spot
They left each other
That first time
Before saying goodbye
Not understanding
There was to be
No face touching or hand holding
For twelve weeks.

A small eternity passed.

One five-year-old boy, chubby and blond, had grown sober
As he waited for the other
On concrete steps
No fidgeting
Dressed nicely
His mother would have been pleased
The other boy, six, lean and brown
Disappeared in the bathroom
Flattening his uncut hair
With his father's grown-up gel
Appeared suddenly
And the boy said, 'Slowpoke,
At last, you've come out!'

He followed his friend
Now taller, older
Regretting the time he said spitefully,
You are *only my neighbour*
Then quick as a comet
They scrambled over the fence together.

Home schooling

Too close to the desk
Now too far
Legs on an angle
Body jangled
Keep still will ya!

Can you blame him?
Everybody virtualised:
Noses gargantuan
Flappy lips
Onslaught of a giddy new world
Keep the phone still for godsake.

Make it fun for him
Parents bicker
You're no help at all
Stressed from doing homework
Working from home I mean

Delighted that
School's in the past
Easily entrapped –
Why can't I see my friends?
Gatherings permitted in 10, no 5, no 2
Keep up please

A sad mouse face
love of my life
Let me give you a hug
See you and touch you
in the flesh
I can't the rest.

What should we do now?

No playground, playdate
Beach or school, and
Despite the cookies we just made
The robots we became
You look glum my boy
As this cubby house collapses
Blankets and pillows over us.

What should I do with you?

Trap you in a story
Where children play
Together
At the playground, on the beach.
Not this all over again.

I know
We both will board a capsule
Fly away in time
Until we can
Make castles of real sand.

1,2,3,4 school kids

One thousand school children in iso;
four of their mates got Covid.

Iso's unlike staying-at-home
playground 'exercising' NOT AN OPTION
instead them kids are on the balcony
blowing bubbles like mad
wishing they could hitch a ride.

Parents start with good intentions:
screen time two hours max
reading one hour, creative arts is fun for all…

Now the internet is our saviour
electricity be the oxygen tank
deliver us from the terror of a power outage.

Day seven.

Words on the pavement

for dad

You asked for two things:
        Your toothbrush, Nani's daily prayer book
A photocopy
We had carried from Delhi
An original home.

While Mum's palm trembled on your inner thigh
The masked soldier
Adjusted his gun, fingers twitching
        'Bloody Kai-Indians! Go now!'
F i v e minutes too long for him
When they kept you for six days and nights
        'The book?' you ask, urgently
I place it in your open palms
A loose page falls in the wind
Escaping
The barbed wire fence
While you – shoved to a backroom
        Another detainee brought in your place –
Remain trapped inside.

The media stalked the compound
Lunging at the visiting wife
Her face full of defeat, heart aquiver
With notebooks and pens
No digital technology back then
It was 1987 after all
Time to tell the world
What just happened?

My mother walked past in a trance:
I spilled the beans
My 18-year-old-life
In a small Pacific paradise
Suddenly becoming important.

What did you do?
       'Your father's a hero.'
         A fool.'
                  'I told him not to get into politics.'
What did they do to you?
You never revealed
They gave you chicken for dinner, you said –
The Pacific way
Did you say that to make me laugh?
You made me cry
When I saw the bruises on your back
The ones you tried to hide
Then forgot to
As you washed yourself
Concealing the barest bits of you
Did it happen when
They separated the ministers?
Fijians on one side, Indians on the other
While you held on tight
A Labour man in a colonial chiefdom
Is that all they had against you?

When they let you go
And you stumbled on the pavement
Into the arms of strangers
Did you see me?
I was waiting in the corner
In the shadow of a coconut palm
A ghoulish crown upon my head
Yet so unimportant was I
Just one in the crowd
Who looked for guidance
And you told us
How you read a daily prayer
To lift the spirits of the others
A Hindu, reading a Christian text –
Morphing from politician to priest
I thought you used to kid around
When Nani read the Bible
In five minutes, you were asleep
But I saw in that moment
Something indefinable:

You were broken but strong.

Finally, you turned
Away from the people
Towards me
Giving me a wad of paper
The daily prayer book; sullied, bent
With an unreadable script – yours
That day you became a poet, so did I
Thirty years later
The same age you were, when
They got you
Then let you go stumbling on the pavement
With only words in your hand.

Based on my experience of the first Fijian coup on 14 May 1987.

Blue skies

If I burst the blue
skin of the sky
near the chest
will I find
a heart?

Or will there only
be layer on layer
of celestial blue
to fall through
and no safety net?

In lockdown

Locked in, locked out
long spikes locked onto
cells, snake-like
air slips deep into the lungs:
a total eclipse of the heart.

Come out, come out
of your cell
to the park to
BREATHE
on your own –

there's a
clamp down
on gatherings,
a multiplication
of floaters
in my eyes.

A ship of shadows
drifts from one colonial port
to another
with great-grandmother's
*mangalsutra**
ripped from the neck
by hands, her own –

seeking freedom
on arrival
in an unknown place
bound by
the chain of indenture.

Generations later
mother left her country too
but on a plane – sheer luxury –
to a place very much on the map
still, her bridal hands were busy
swatting island mosquitos
bumping baby skin.

Father became a politician
with a gun to his head
in the country of his birth
some battles you just can't win:
we left again.

Old parents
sit in a suburban garage
like twin cars
forced to social distance
from children standing in the rain
holding onto severed
umbilical cord, while
a portion remains inside
the womb, that first home,
like memory in a refugee,
resurrecting.

---

* *Mangalsutra* is a chain worn by Indian women that identifies them as married.

Bat wing

We will do what is
feared by many
but which you are
more afraid of naturally.

We will be alone, lonely
live obscured by a bat wing
some, facing death perhaps.

You will become host-less, single
made wild with hunger
forced to die off.

Then, we'll be there
in plain sight
and you won't
when the wings fold finally.

Shooting star

An ambulance streaks past
Like a shooting star
Carrying in its rocky cradle
A heart patient
The diagnosis is:
Heartbreak –
Burnt up from loneliness.

Nani

A-1/177 Safdarjung Enclave.
Not quite the Taj Mahal
But still very much
A memory of love
Like all objects and things
Greater than itself.

In the palm of my hand curls
Strands from a cotton pouch
And I think of her luscious hair
Dropping
Like a waterfall
Down the cliff
Of her back.

I dip my finger in
An empty Ponds jar
And I remember her skin
The colour of creamy caramel
With grooves and edges.

The frilly bible cover quivers
When a favourite line appears like
Braille beneath my fingers:
Thy word is a lamp unto my feet, and
A light unto my path
Flicking Jesus in my mind
Like carrom coins into pockets.

Her cotton-thin nightie
Unravels on my body
Encasing it with an emptiness   because
Everything's her really
But she's not here.

Daffodils

A golden halo
In one spot of the garden
Where my parents commune
Staving off mid-winter blues.

I didn't know
Daffodils grew at this time
In that half-year of separation
I missed my mother's embrace
Her giving, trembling hands
My father's offerings:
A book, an item of clothing
All those parts of one that couldn't touch.

'So many birds come to the front yard,'
My mum and dad say cheerfully
Trying to make a lonely landscape whole again
I don't see any
Only a red wheelbarrow
And a dalliance of daffodils.

I leave my seat by the window
To make my parents cups of tea
Oh wait! A singing blackbird
It's narrow yellow eye-ring
Encircling orbs of light
Bright faces like my family.

Family WhatsApp

Tumble in trivia
Familywhatsappchat
I'm all ears
Literally holding on to hear
Which NetflixFoxtel series you binge-watched all night
What 'lockdown sauce' you manufactured for the family lunch
And the names of the new plants in your garden.

In my home, food is bland, laughter is descending notes
The balcony plants are a row of droopy eyelids;

I could do with a booster.

Fred Hollows' gully

for Maria

In the heart of the suburb
grows a gully
a leafy, mossy place
of soft and scattered light
flickering on a footbridge
over pebbled creek.

In the middle of this chasm
a hollowed tree stood
purposeful for a boy
sharpening his gully stick
home for bird and insect alone
it seemed at first
then as if suddenly
at base of sacred trunk emerged
a door, red and so small,
fit for a leprechaun if at all
stirred a cavernous longing
to exit from this covid world.

A host of virtual images
they zoom upon that inward eye –
your mask put aside
hair combed neat in preparation
black cardigan holding your heart
solid shoes that stopped you falling
as you travelled through the eulogy
of your brother's life –

they bring me back
like a thunderclap
from this ecosystem of escape
to this world we share
the one I love so much.

Oh subterranean space
You restore my sight.

Woman in the park

Little lockdown families
In pockets of the park.

Ball, bat, frisbee
A trident against lethargy.

Your ball slips from your hands,
Settles at my feet.

We exchange a smile:
An invisible barrier breaks brief.

I swear I heard a sigh,
That in your soul begins.

Before I leave the park
I see you on a swing.

Your baby at a distance
Wishing for a different time.

The aching sunshine
Washes over your open palms.

Angel

Your hair is
a brightly lit field of corn –
both silk and tassel.

Can you be our celestial intermediary?
Your head bowed down so low,
your wings folded in.

Eighteen months passed,
we began to accept
these feelings of suspense:
When would our husbands be
without anxiety
our parents without fear
When would our children see
the outside world once more.

Barely there benevolence
fades into oblivion
just before
you unlock and whisper:
I hope it gets better soon.

Eight squares of stained glass

I've neglected you lately Lord
Believed I was cruising more than most
Now I'm looking up
At eight squares of light
From the outside and far below
Your grandeur safe and secure
In brick façade, steepled iron cross
Even the sun you command
Radiates through
Squares of primary colours –
Red, yellow, blue
Sparkling in our darkness
In particles of sunshine, dust and air
Your energy is everywhere.

Vertigo

If I were to express my anxiety
in its brightest intensity
I would not tell you about
a girl falling off a flight of stairs,
I would hold up a placard
with two squares:
yellow and red
lines diffused
shapes that didn't allow you to define space
and made you seasick without grace.

Never Before

Never has a bright smile, a hearty laugh
turned vicious on an exposed face.

Never has a close contact, a familiar person or place
made you as regretful.

Never have we unknowingly
exposed ourselves and our neighbours –
the butcher, the bakery, and the delicatessen.

Never has air
tasted this delicious.

Never have you been
given a metre of space on the footpath.

Never has your appetite
grown in virulence.

Never have your parents been that far
your children, too near.

Never have you felt so at sea.

Playing Robinson Crusoe

I'll build a bed of grass
wrap rags around my ankles, walk through reeds before sunrise
I'm pretty good at climbing: coconut utensils covered
and swimming too, so fish steaks for dinner eh.
I'll light the fire with my vanity mirror, you know the one that –
when we were together – made you ask provocatively,
'What are you looking for anyway?'

I think we're all looking hard in the mirror now.

God's providence
provides us with the place – our island in the sun –
and the circumstances: virus, lockdown, isolation, sickness, death
to learn the divine lesson of life
learnt anything yet?
maybe…

Before you can make a raft
escaping this wretched world
beware of wild animals
worse, the cravings of your beastly nature
surging involuntarily like they did
on that night when Jekyll became Hyde,
for a seated restaurant meal
a served cappuccino, and a
mouthy exchange with friends.

Separation, as you discover, is really not your thing.

Two Haiku

Numbers

Millions more now gone
Two from Wuhan to Milan
A single fight flown

Corona

You tarty fellow
Wedge of lemon stuck in neck
King coronated

We are all in this together

The federal ministers are proselytising
health and economic goals
While the kookaburras are cracking up
on power poles.
Worboys apple cheeks are red delicious
after infringements peak
While Gladys's green shoots are stagnant
as the virus leaks.
Easterners are frolicking on the beach
While Westerners are being arrested on the street.
In selfless lunity
we are too much in the community.
But do not be afraid for
We are all in this together.

Do the hokey pokey

Tom first puts his left foot in
Charles puts his left foot out
Boris puts his left foot in
And they shake them all about
Donald does the hokey pokey
And turns the world around
That's what it's all about!

A normal day

At the end of the day
when the world has cooled down
passions have lost point
light turns softly into darkness
I gaze upon my son
laughing at the screen
resisting bedtime
his father busy in the background
and I wonder – is this a good life?

I wash the dirty dishes
throw out lazy leftovers
on top of tags
cut neatly off clothes
the ones that make you itchy and angry
then I know
things feel almost normal.

Takeaway pie with tomato sauce

A pie with tomato sauce please
proved hard to resist.
Bounding homeward
I stopped on empty side-walk
gave into temptation
bit into
hot chicken-mushroom pie
more appetising than an apple,
let my mask dangle off cowardly chin
squirted red sauce also
onto footpath.
Seconds later, a person passed by
so near wearing naked mouth
it seemed, he too was eating my pie.
Alarmed, I consumed with haste
and terrible guilt
blinking away chastising looks.
I returned home finally
the pie wholly consumed
gave me a look of innocence
or so I thought.
My mask had betrayed me so easily…
Out damn spot!
Treacherous tomato sauce.

Return to what remains

Curve your mouth upwards
let teeth, tongue, gums gloriously display
return to laughter.

Untie your hair
throw away the ribbon
return to hanging your hair low.

Press your palms on bark
let feet on roots lightly tread
return to your favourite fig tree.

Hold his hand
feel its warm roughness
return to love.

Reach for the heights
let arms in sky take off
return to your imagination.

See the sun's light in the distance
watch twilight approach; nature's ambiguity
return to your humanity.

To what remains.

www.ingramcontent.com/pod-product-compliance
Lightning Source LLC
Chambersburg PA
CBHW070338120526
44590CB00017B/2936